HAL LEONARD

GUITAR METHOD

ROCK GUITAR SONGS

T0081553

PLAYBACK+
Speed • Pitch • Balance • Loop

To access audio visit:
www.halleonard.com/mylibrary

Enter Code
5037-3262-3254-8272

ISBN 978-1-4234-1774-3

HAL•LEONARD®

Visit Hal Leonard Online at
www.halleonard.com

Contact us:
Hal Leonard
7777 West Bluemound Road
Milwaukee, WI 53213
Email: info@halleonard.com

In Europe, contact:
Hal Leonard Europe Limited
42 Wigmore Street
Marylebone, London, W1U 2RN
Email: info@halleonardeurope.com

In Australia, contact:
Hal Leonard Australia Pty. Ltd.
4 Lentara Court
Cheltenham, Victoria, 3192 Australia
Email: info@halleonard.com.au

Ain't Talkin' 'Bout Love

Words and Music by David Lee Roth, Edward Van Halen, Alex Van Halen and Michael Anthony

Tune down 1/2 step:
(low to high) Eb-Ab-Db-Gb-Bb-Eb

Intro

Moderate Rock ♩ = 138

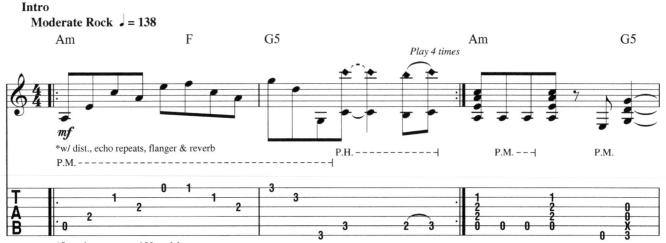

*w/ dist., echo repeats, flanger & reverb

*Set echo at approx. 100ms delay.
Set flanger for slow speed w/ regeneration sweep and moderate depth.

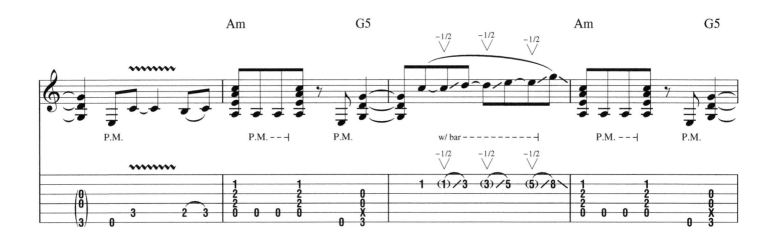

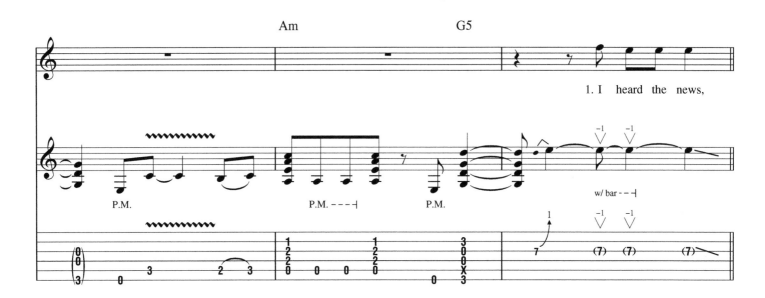

1. I heard the news,

*Hold bend while sliding.

Guitar Solo

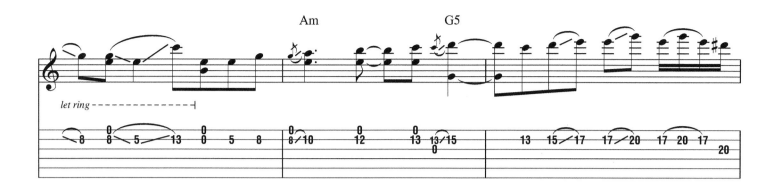

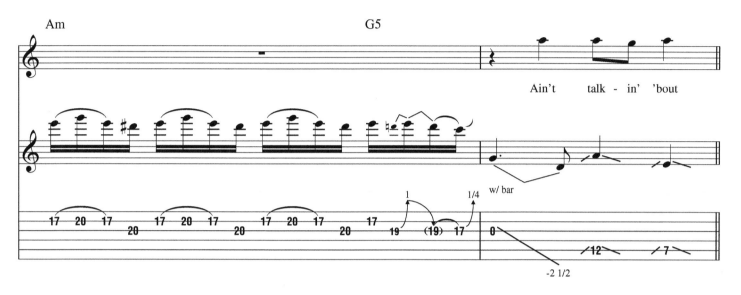

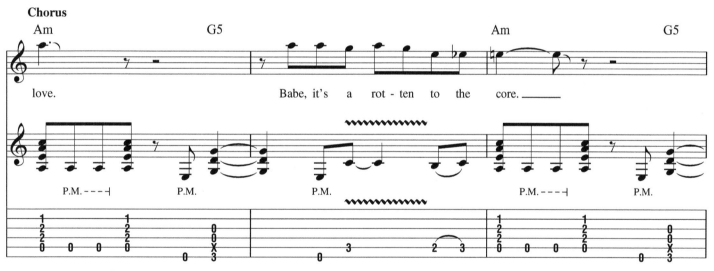

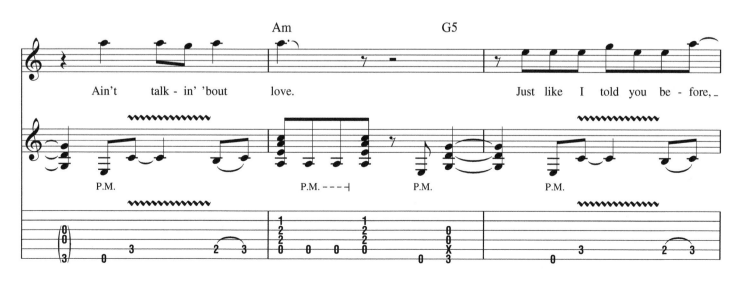

*Lower vol. knob about halfway to produce a slightly distorted tone.

Interlude

Pitch: D G B

Additional Lyrics

2. You know you're semi good lookin',
   And on the streets again.
   Oh, yeah, you think you're really cookin', baby.
   You better find yourself a friend, my friend.

Rock and Roll All Nite

Words and Music by Paul Stanley and Gene Simmons

Tune down 1/2 step:
(low to high) Eb–Ab–Db–Gb–Bb–Eb

Intro

Moderately fast Rock ♩ = 142

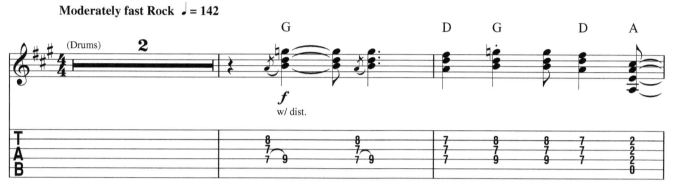

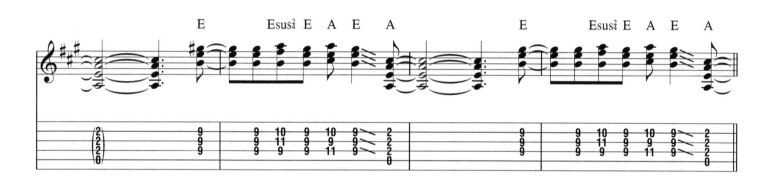

Verse

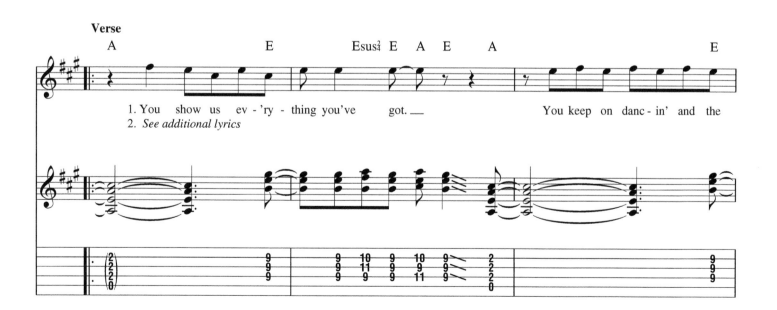

1. You show us ev - 'ry - thing you've got. ___ You keep on danc - in' and the
2. *See additional lyrics*

and par-ty ev-er-y day. I wan-na rock and roll all nite

and par-ty ev-er-y day.

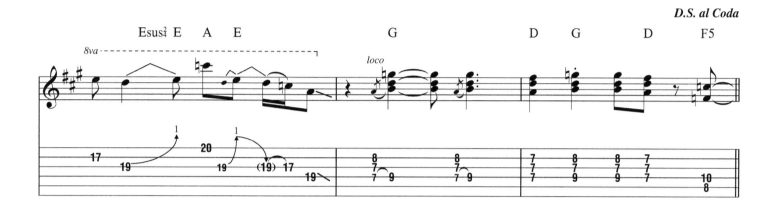

D.S. al Coda

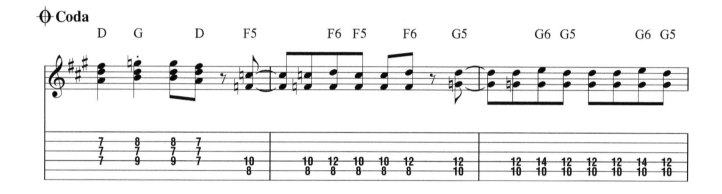

Additional Lyrics

2. You keep on sayin' you'll be mine for awhile.
You're looking fancy and I like your style.
And you drive us wild; we'll drive you crazy.
And you show us ev'rything you've got.
Well, baby, baby, that's quite a lot.
And you drive us wild; we'll drive you crazy.

Brown Eyed Girl

Words and Music by Van Morrison

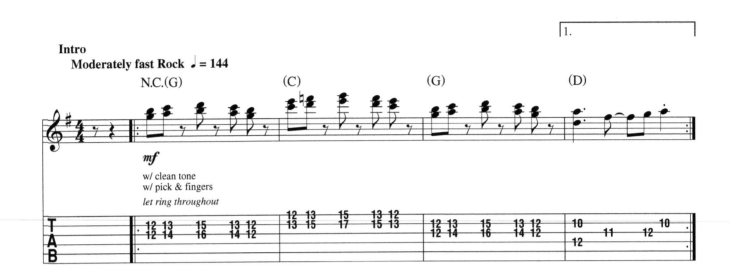

1. Hey, where did we go ___ days ___ when the rains ___

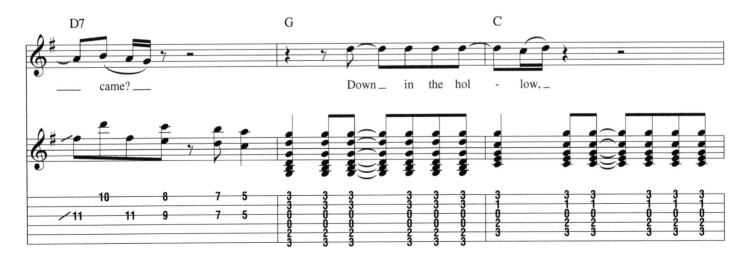

___ came? ___ Down ___ in the hol - low, ___

Verse

2. Now, what - ev - er hap - pened to Tues - day and so ___ slow?

Go - ing down the old ___ mine ___ with a

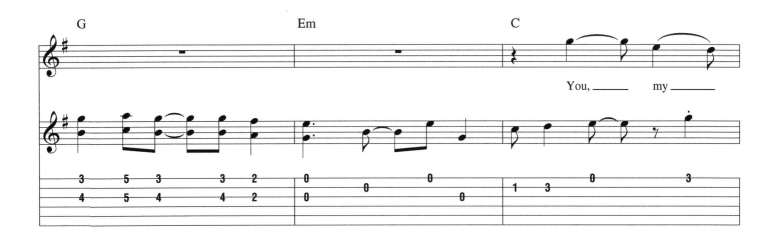

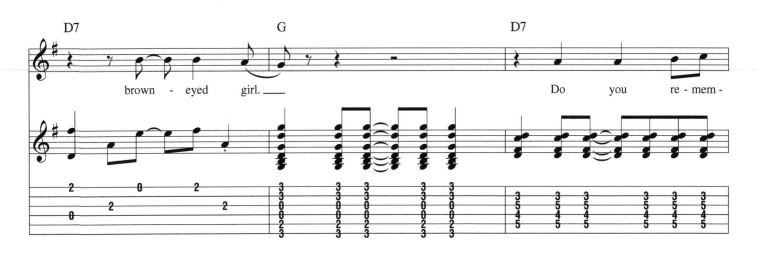

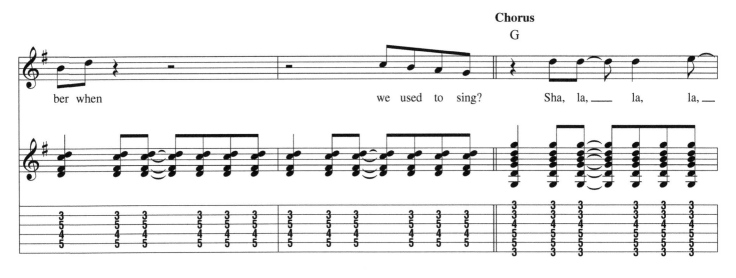

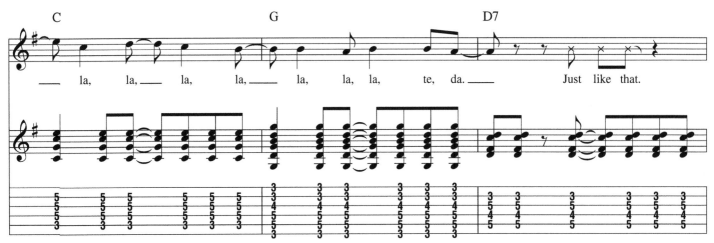

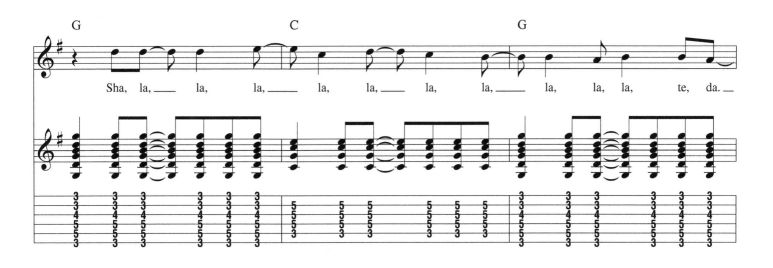

Sha, la,___ la, la,___ la, la,___ la, la,___ la, la, la, te, da.__

La, te, da._

Bass Interlude

N.C.(G) (C) (G) (D7)

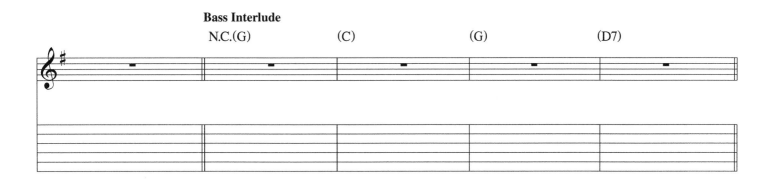

Verse

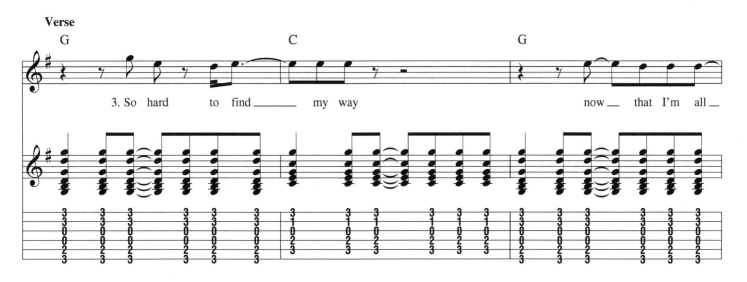

3. So hard to find_____ my way now__ that I'm all__

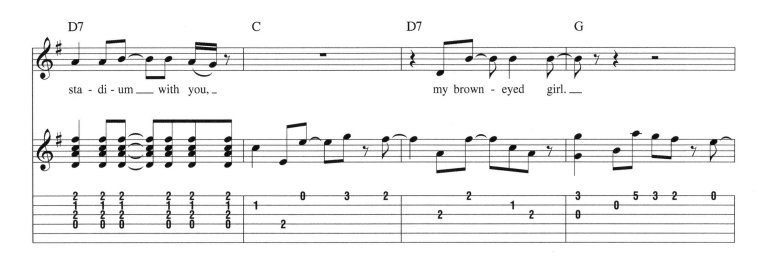

sta - di - um ___ with you, ___ my brown - eyed girl. ___

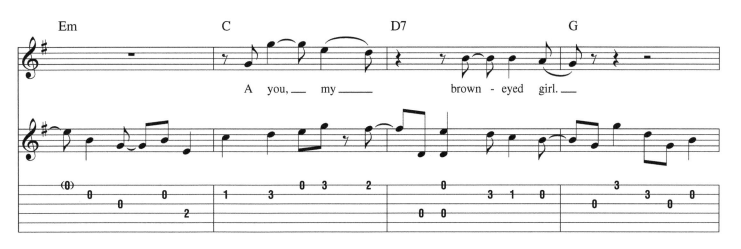

A you, ___ my ___ brown - eyed girl. ___

Do you re - mem - ber when, a, we used to sing?

Play 4 times & fade

Chorus

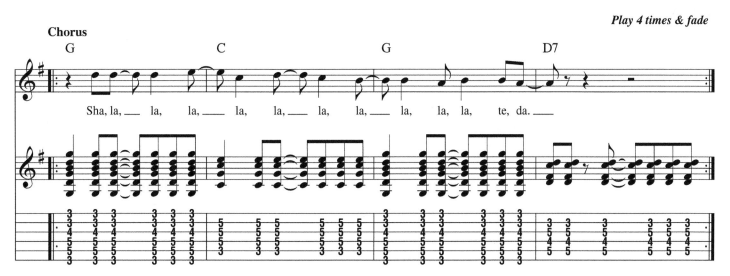

Sha, la, ___ la, la, ___ la, la, ___ la, la, ___ la, la, la, te, da. ___

Get Back

Words and Music by John Lennon and Paul McCartney

Intro
Moderate Rock ♩ = 123

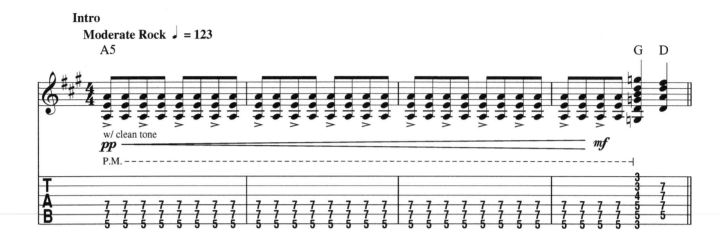

% Verse

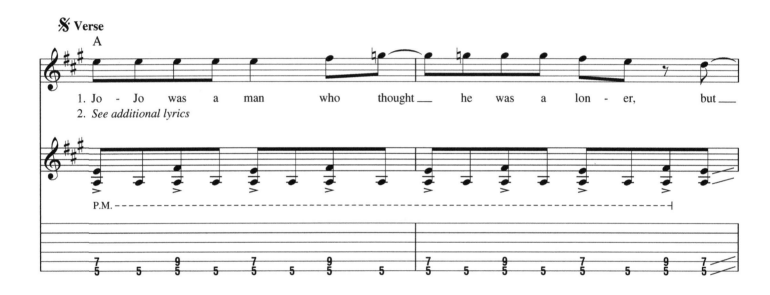

1. Jo - Jo was a man who thought __ he was a lon - er, but __
2. *See additional lyrics*

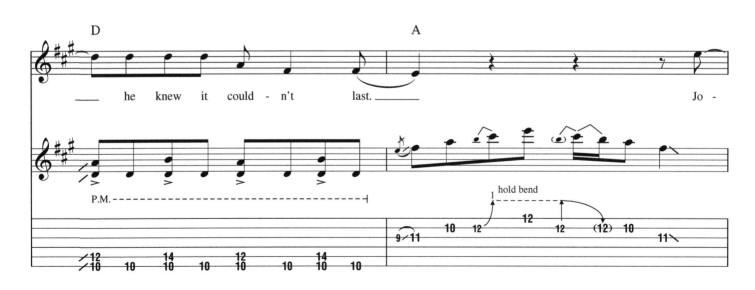

__ he knew it could - n't last. __

Jo -

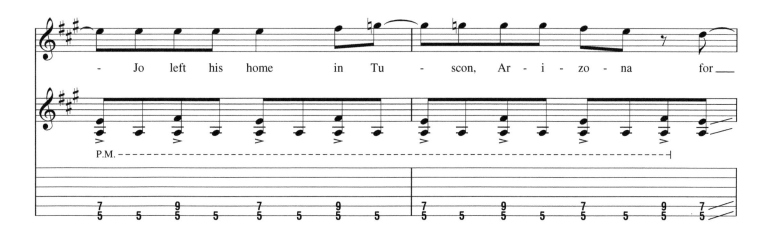

-Jo left his home in Tu - scon, Ar - i - zo - na   for ___

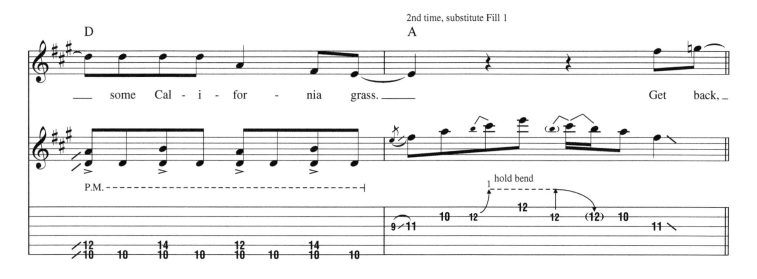

D   2nd time, substitute Fill 1   A

___ some Cal - i - for - nia grass. ___   Get   back, ___

Chorus
A7

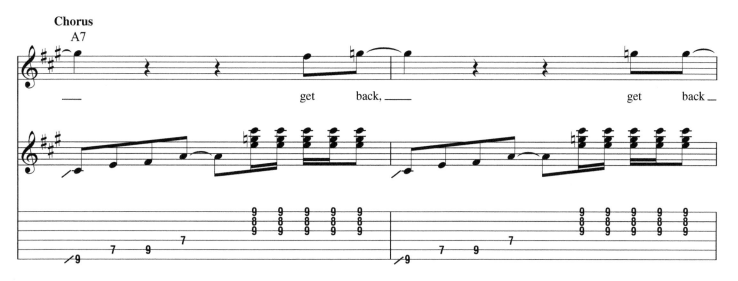

___   get   back, ___   get   back ___

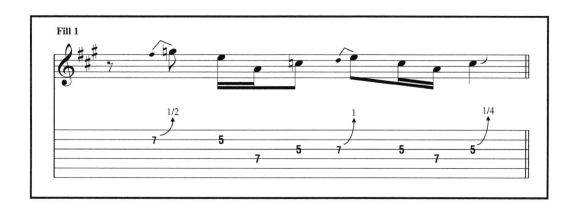

Fill 1

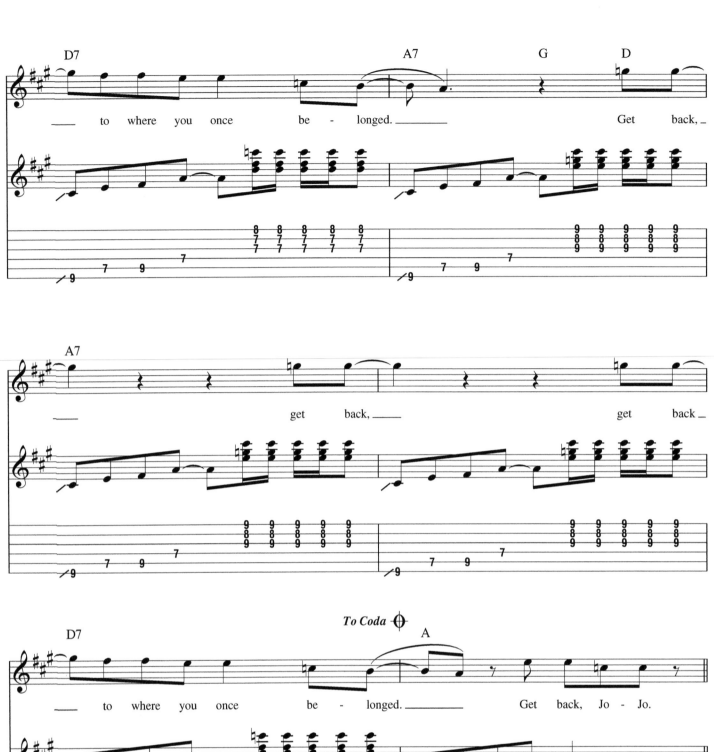

to where you once be - longed. _____ Get back, _

get back, _____ get back _

To Coda ⊕

to where you once be - longed. _____ Get back, Jo - Jo.

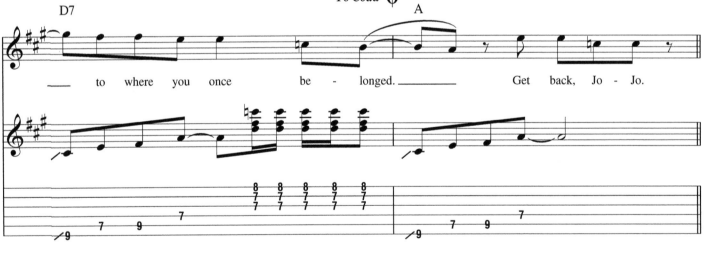

Guitar Solo

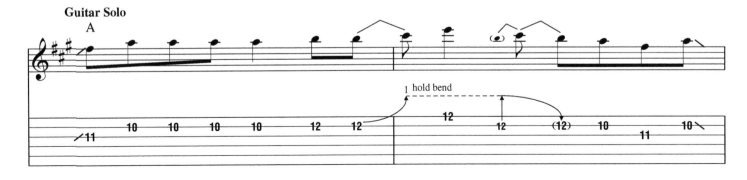

1 hold bend

26

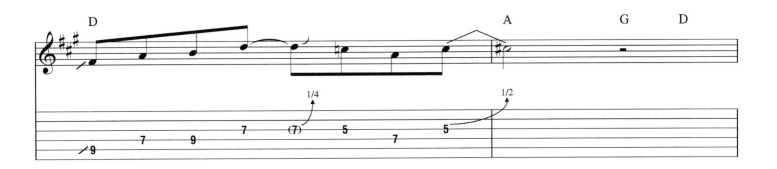

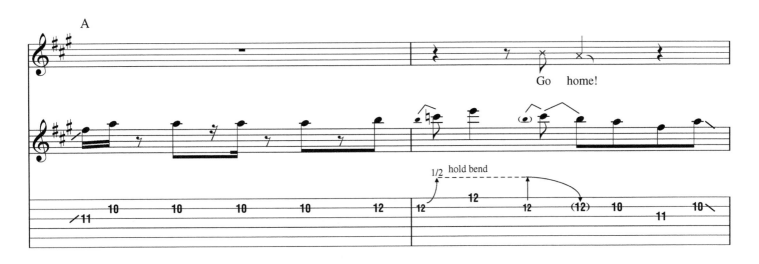

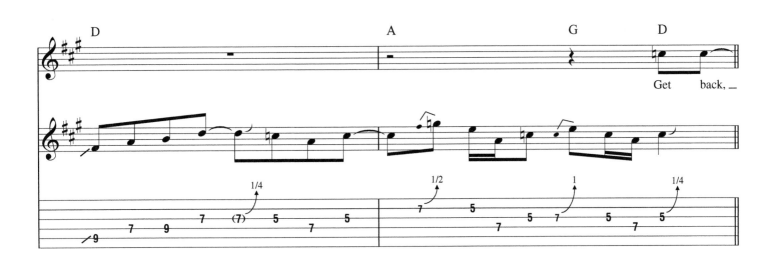

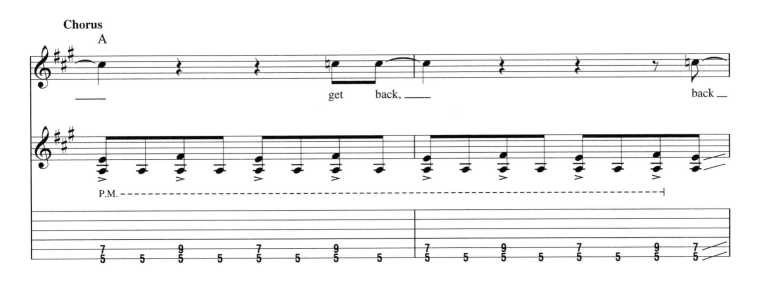

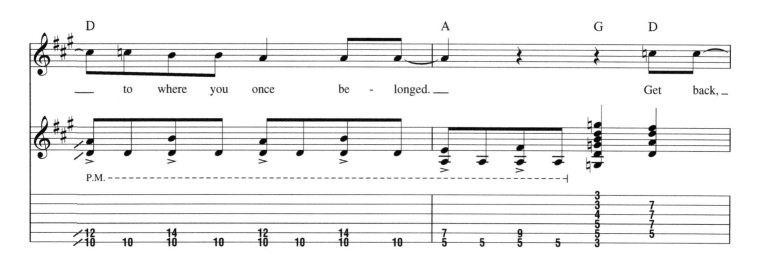

— to where you once be - longed. —   Get back, —

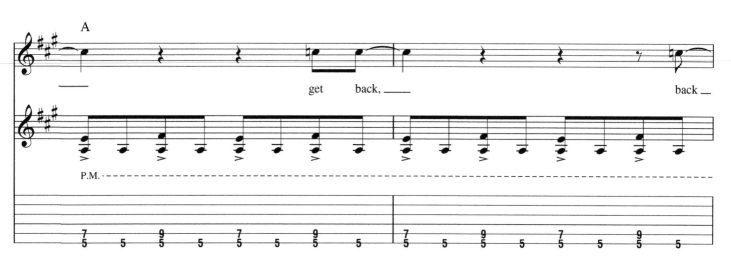

—   get back, ——   back —

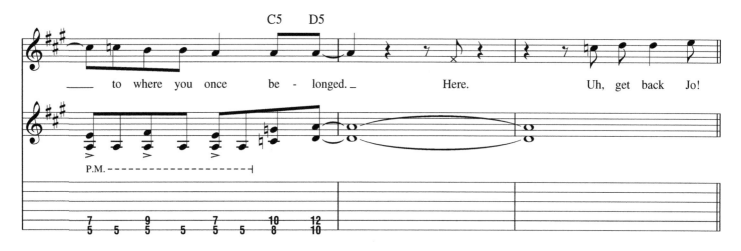

— to where you once be - longed. —   Here.   Uh, get back Jo!

Piano Solo

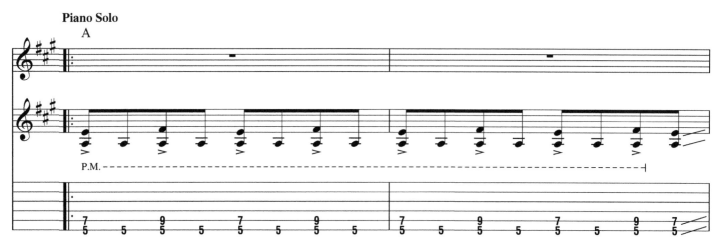

⊕ **Coda**

Guitar Solo

Get back, Lor - et - ta.

hold bend

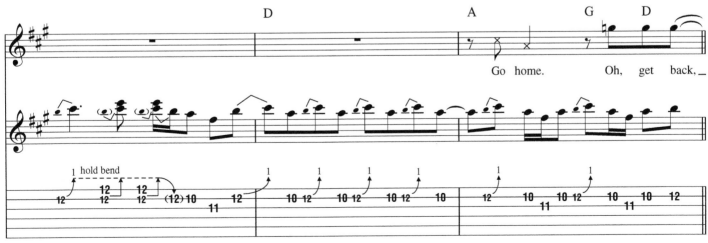

Go home.   Oh,   get   back, ___

hold bend

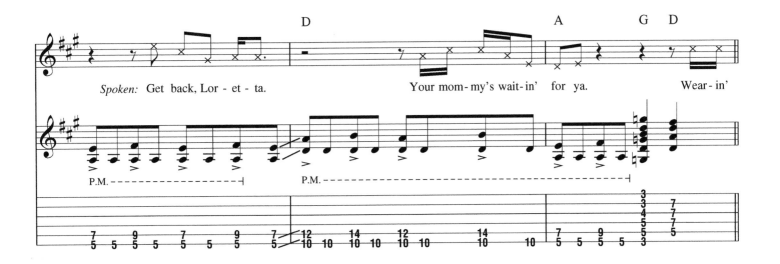

Spoken: Get back, Lor - et - ta.

Your mom- my's wait-in' for ya.

Wear- in'

her high - heel shoes

and her low - necked sweat - er.

Repeat and fade

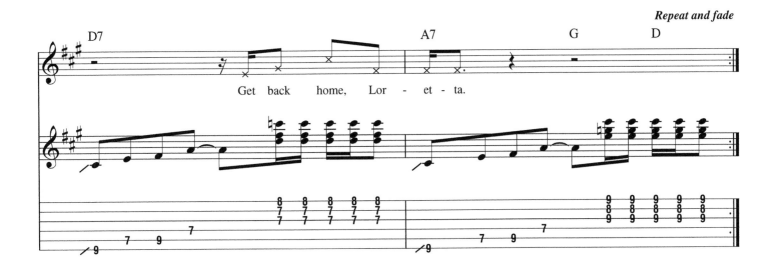

Get back home, Lor - et - ta.

Additional Lyrics

2. Sweet Loretta Martin thought she was a woman
But she was another man.
All the girls around her say she's got it coming
But she gets it while she can.

Scar Tissue

Words and Music by Anthony Kiedis, Flea, John Frusciante and Chad Smith

Chorus

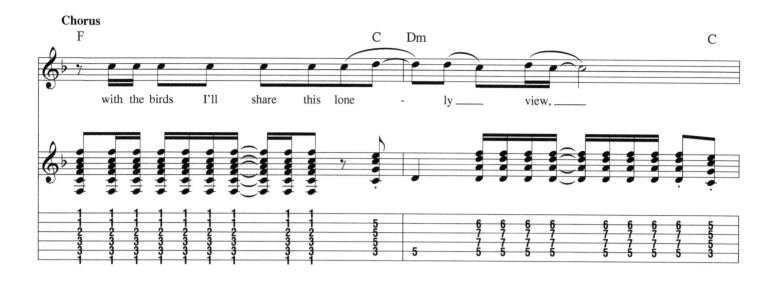

with the birds I'll share this lone - ly ____ view, ____

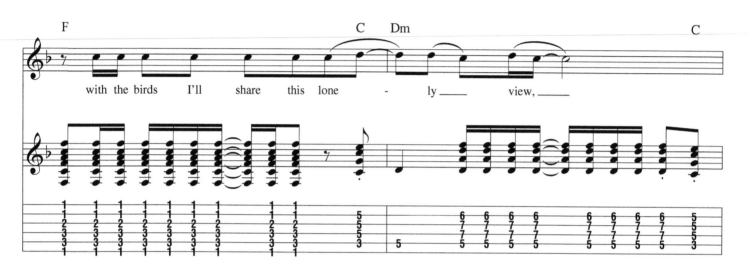

with the birds I'll share this lone - ly ____ view, ____

with the birds I'll share this lone - ly view. _____

w/ slide
w/ pick

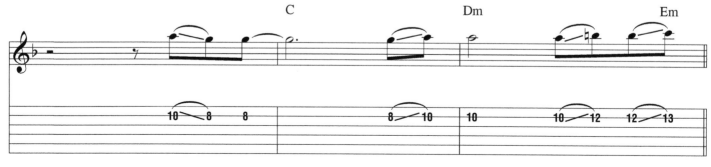

Ah, close your eyes and I'll ___ kiss you, 'cause ___ with the birds I'll share, ___

Chorus

with the birds I'll share this lone - ly ___ view, ___

with the birds I'll share this lone - ly ___ view, ___

with the birds I'll share this lone - ly view. ___

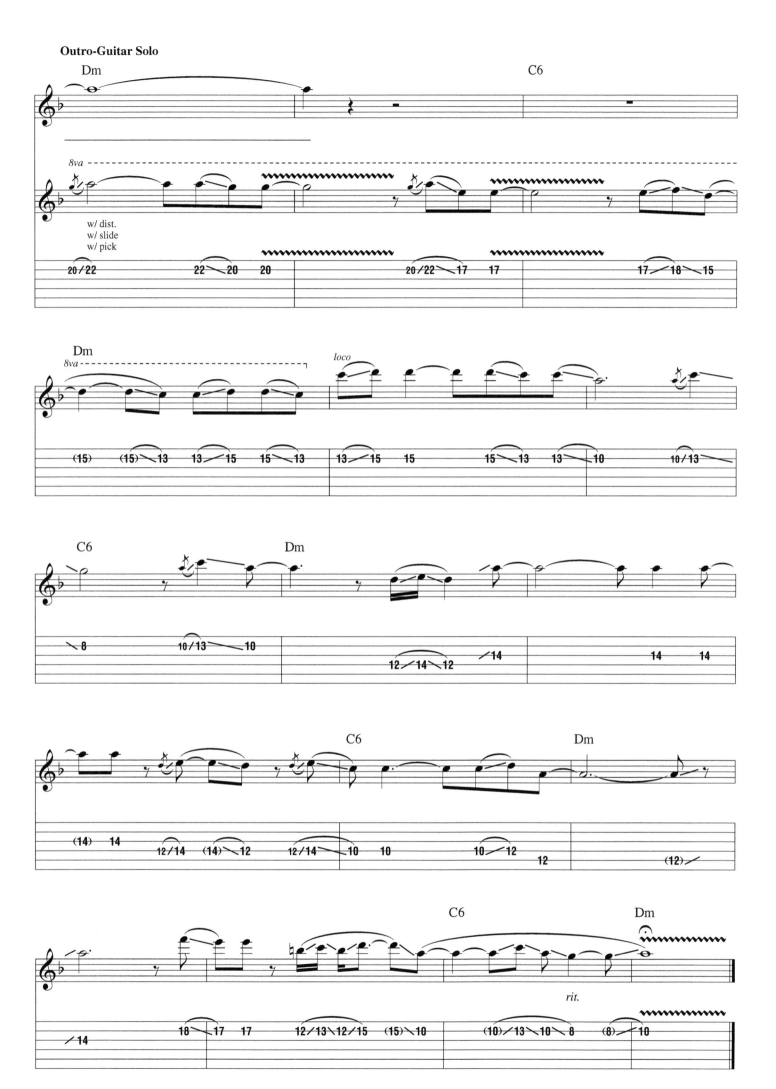

Outro-Guitar Solo

Smells Like Teen Spirit

Words and Music by Kurt Cobain, Krist Novoselic and Dave Grohl

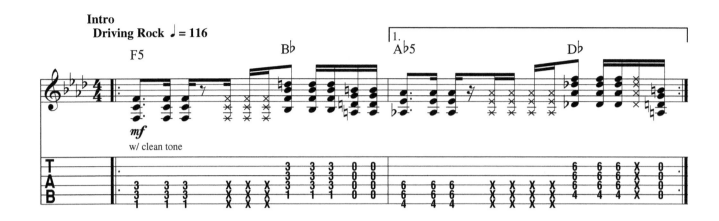

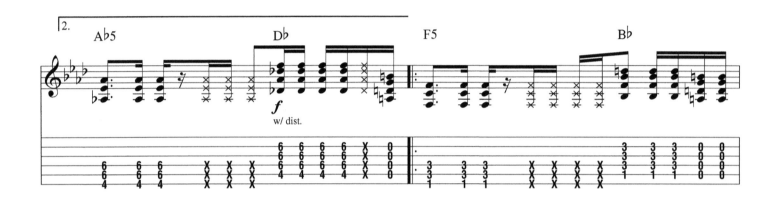

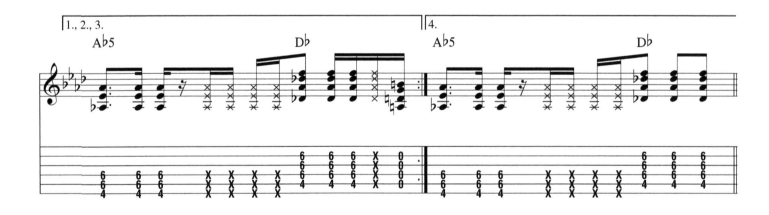

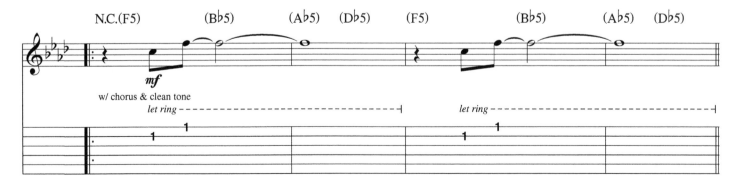

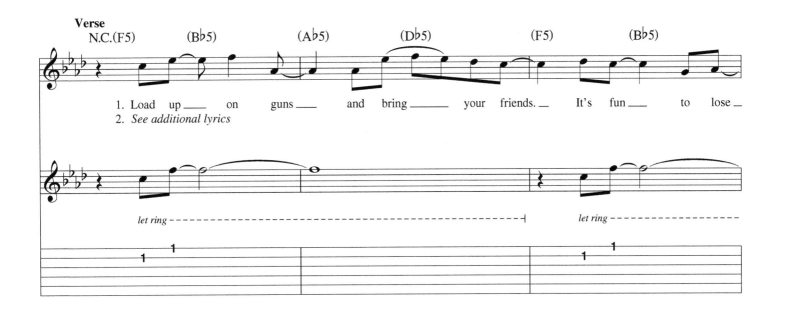

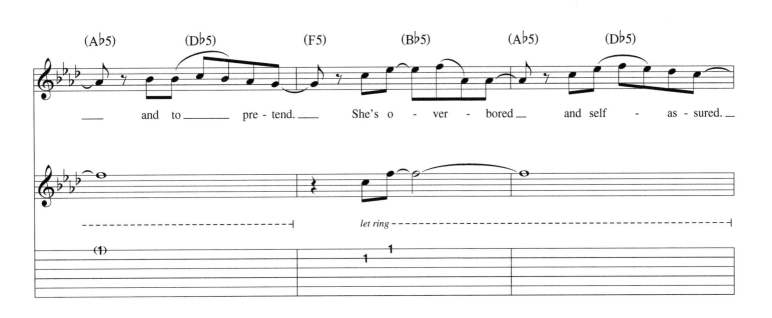

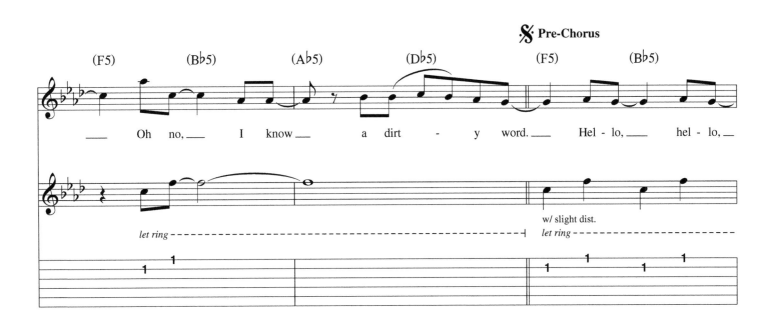

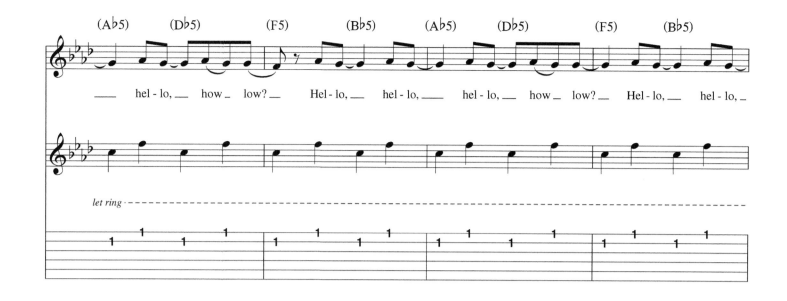

hel - lo, how low? Hel - lo, hel - lo, hel - lo, how low? Hel - lo, hel - lo,

let ring

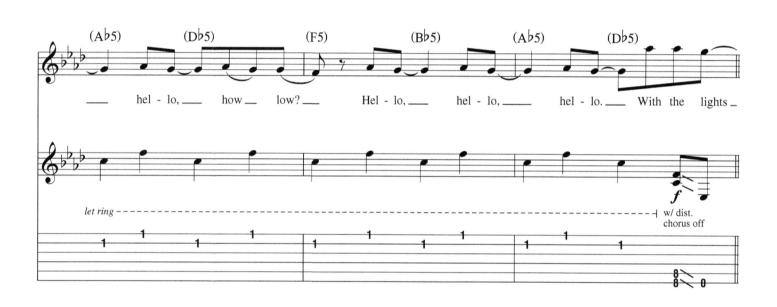

hel - lo, how low? Hel - lo, hel - lo, hel - lo. With the lights

let ring

w/ dist.
chorus off

Chorus

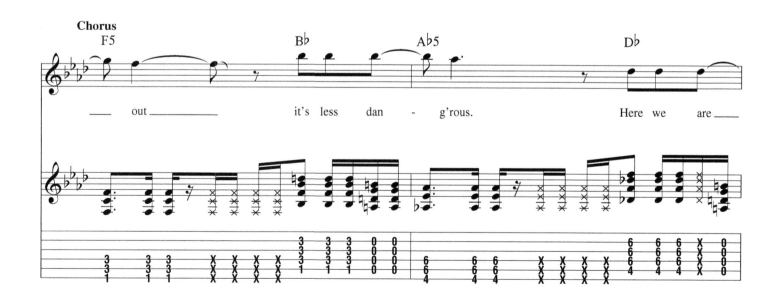

out it's less dan - g'rous. Here we are

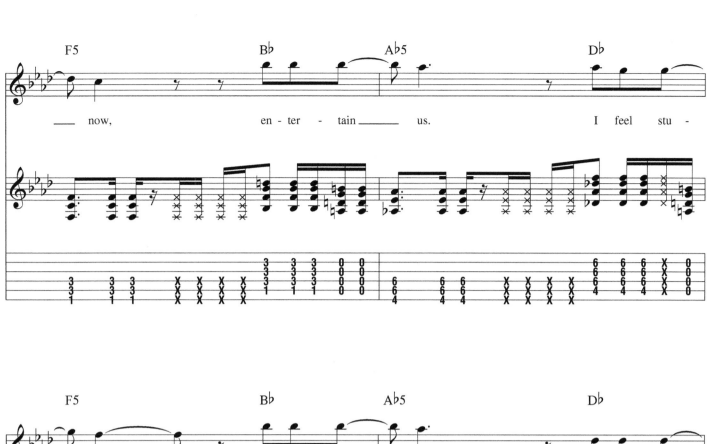

now, en - ter - tain us. I feel stu -

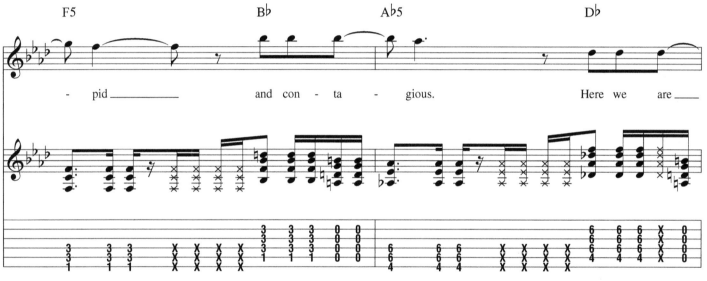

- pid and con - ta - gious. Here we are

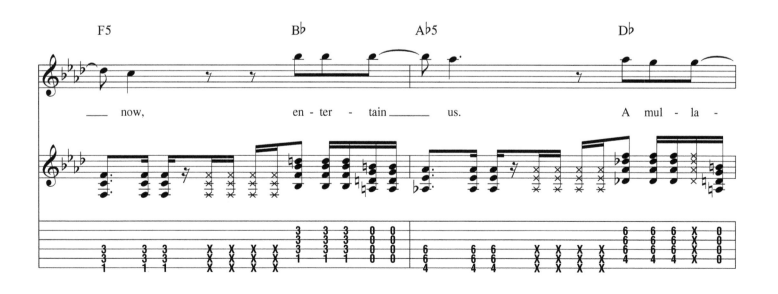

now, en - ter - tain us. A mul - la -

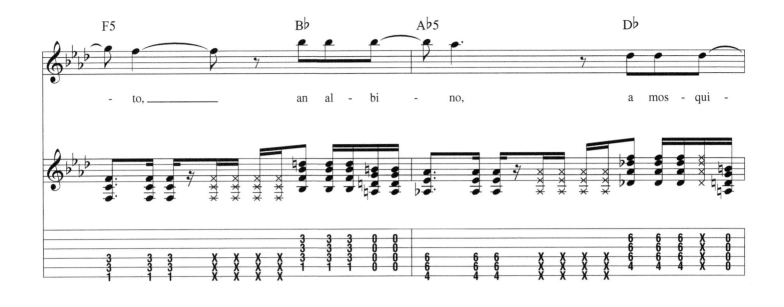

- to, _____ an al - bi - no, a mos - qui -

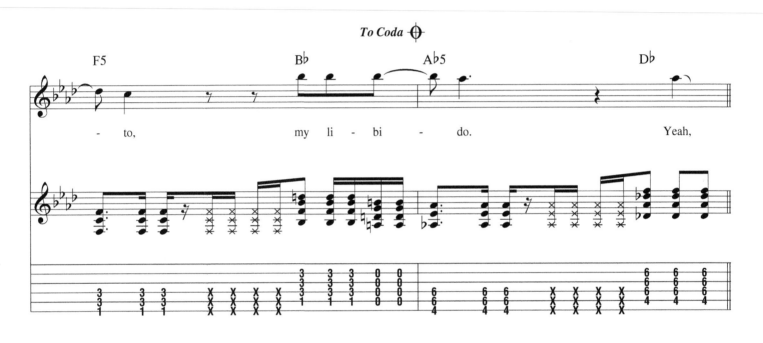

To Coda ⊕

- to, my li - bi - do. Yeah,

Bridge

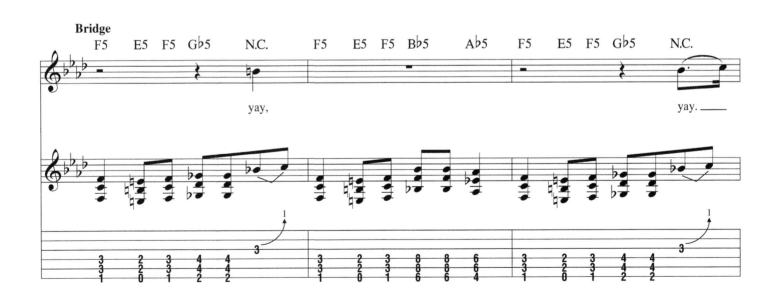

yay, yay. ____

Additional Lyrics

2. I'm worse at what I do best,
   And for this gift I feel blessed.
   Our little group has always been
   And always will until the end.

Smoke on the Water

Words and Music by Ritchie Blackmore, Ian Gillan, Roger Glover, Jon Lord and Ian Paice

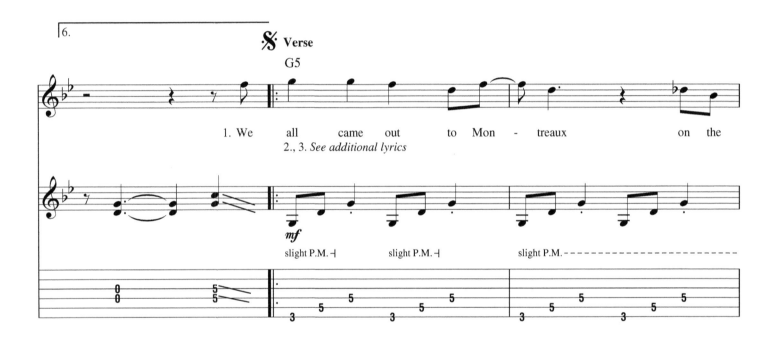

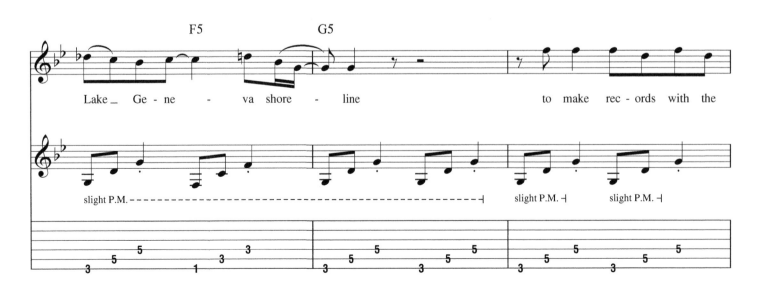

mo - bile, _____ we did - n't have much time. _____

But Frank Zap - pa and the Moth - ers _____ were at the best place a - round. _____

_____ But some stu - pid with a flare gun

Chorus

burned the place to the _____ ground. _____ Smoke on the

wa - ter,   a   fire ___ in   the   sky. ___

To Coda ⊕

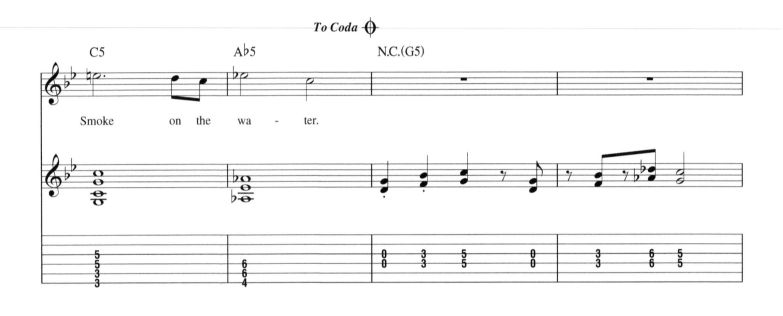

Smoke   on   the   wa - ter.

1.   2.

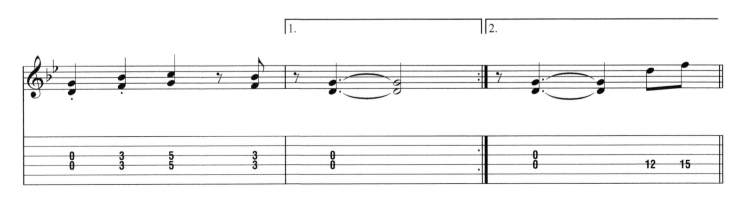

Guitar Solo

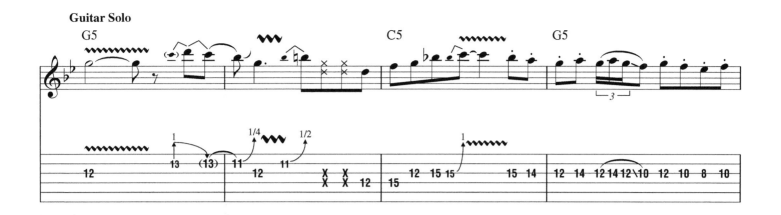

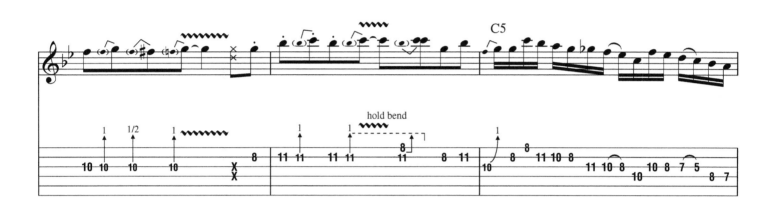

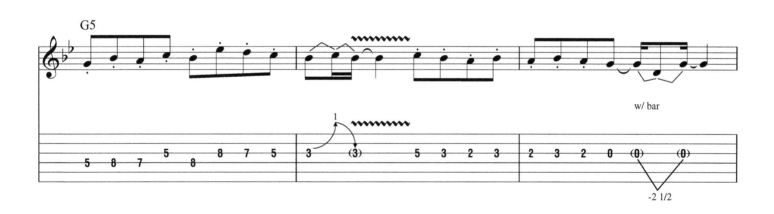

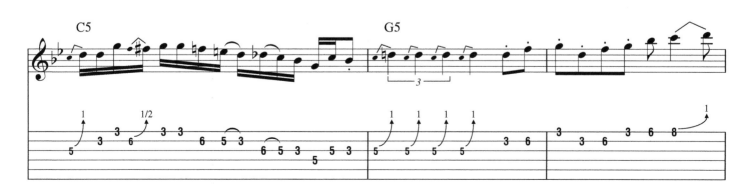

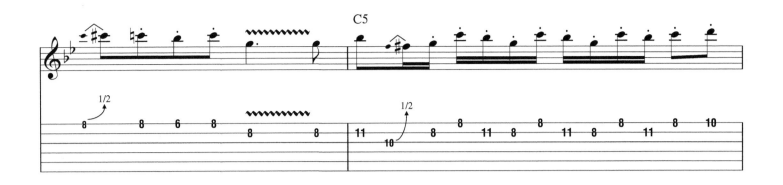

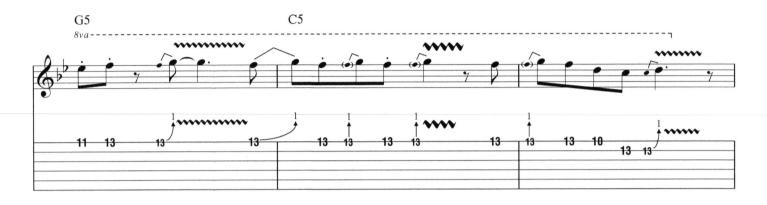

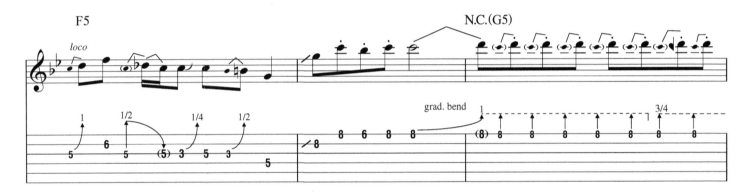

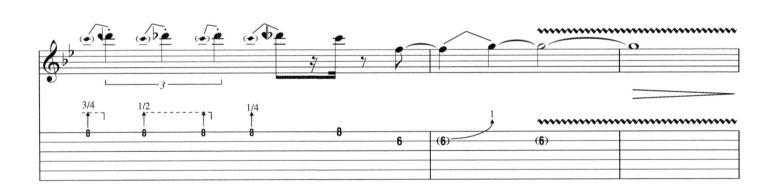

Coda

Outro-Organ Solo

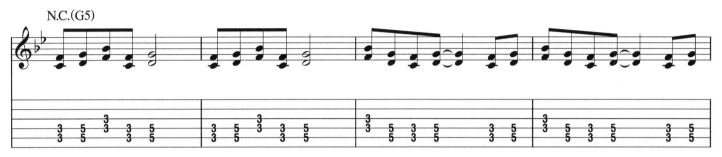

Begin fade

Fade out

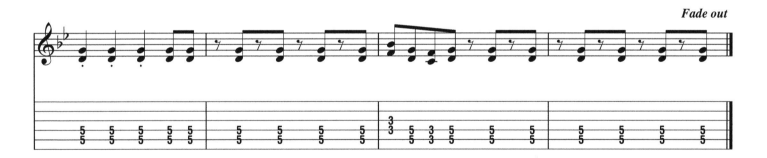

Additional Lyrics

2. They burned down the gambling house,
   It died with an awful sound.
   A Funky Claude was running in and out,
   Pulling kids out the ground.
   When it all was over, we had to find another place.
   But Swiss time was running out;
   It seemed we would lose the race.

3. We ended up at the Grand Hotel,
   It was empty, cold and bare.
   But with the Rolling truck Stones thing just outside,
   Making our music there.
   With a few red lights, a few old beds
   We made a place to sweat.
   No matter what we get out of this,
   I know, I know we'll never forget.

Sweet Home Alabama

Words and Music by Ronnie Van Zant, Ed King and Gary Rossington

*Key signature denotes D Mixolydian.

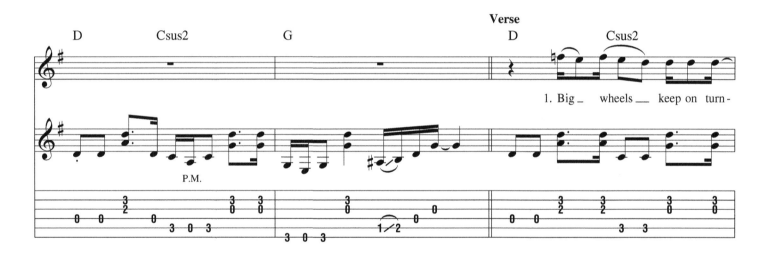

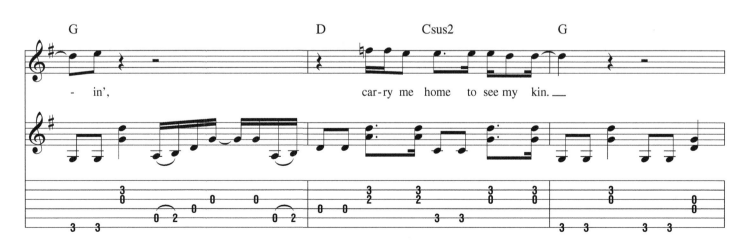

Well, I hope Neil Young will re-mem - ber,   a south-ern man _ don't need him a-

Chorus

round,   an - y-how.   Sweet _ home   Al - a - bam - a,

where the skies   are   so blue. __   Sweet _ home   Al - a-

bam - a,   Lord, I'm com-in' home   to you.

Guitar Solo

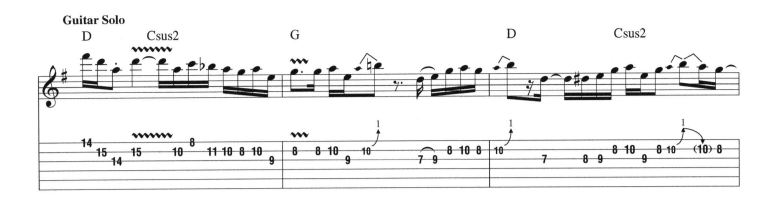

Verse

3. In Bir-ming-ham _ they love the gov - 'nor, boo, boo,

w/ bar

hoo. Now we all did _ what we could do. Now Wa-ter - gate _ does not

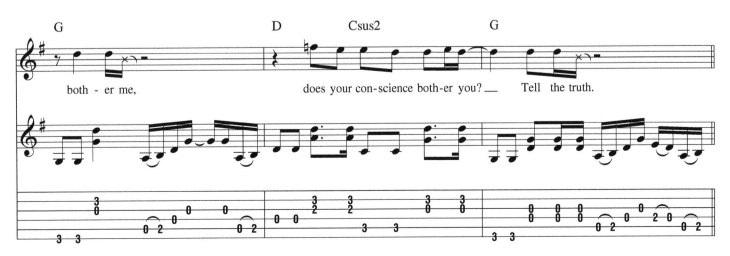

both - er me, does your con-science both-er you? _ Tell the truth.

Chorus

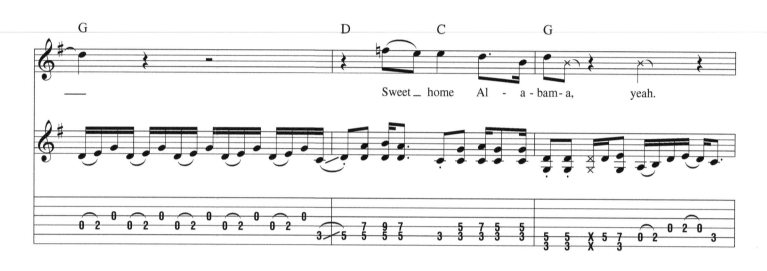

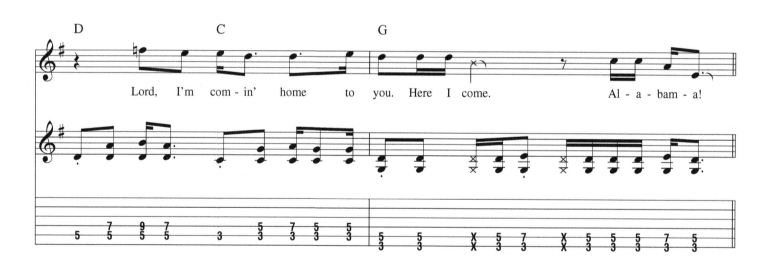

Guitar Solo

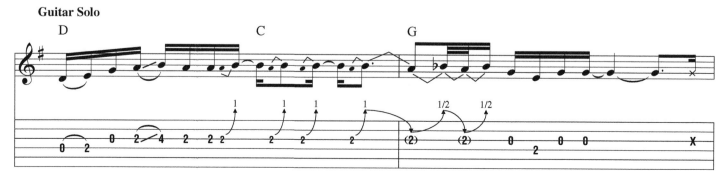

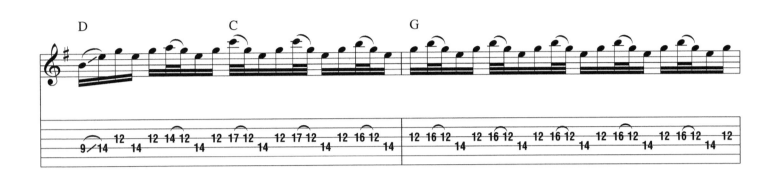

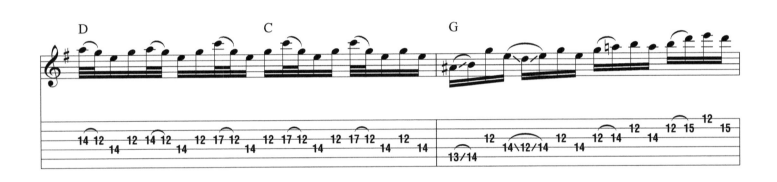

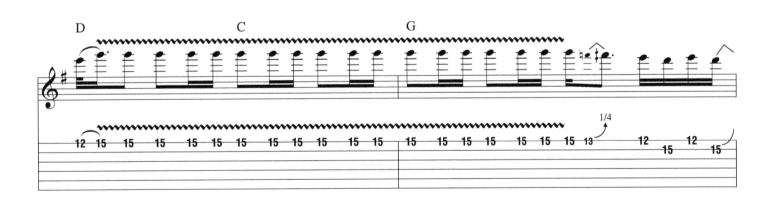

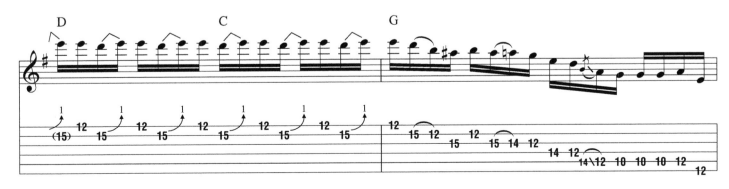

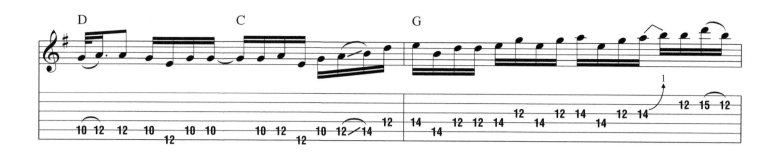

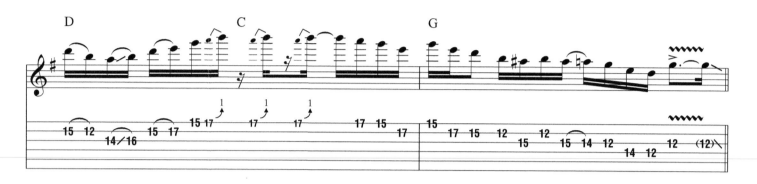

Interlude

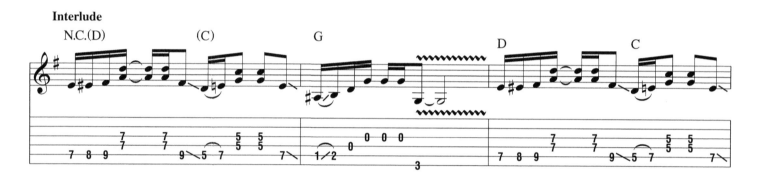

Verse

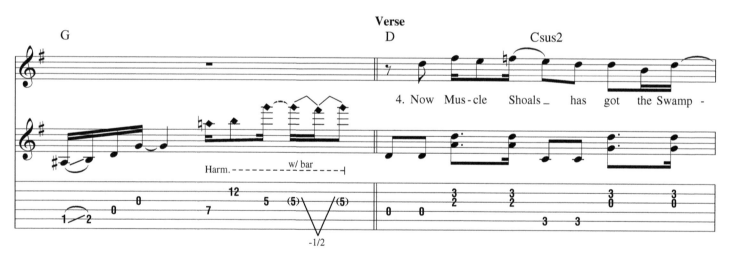

4. Now Mus-cle Shoals _ has got the Swamp -

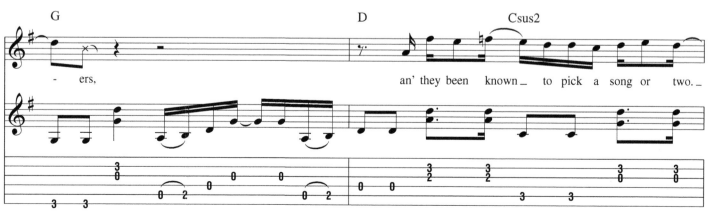

- ers, an' they been known _ to pick a song or two. _

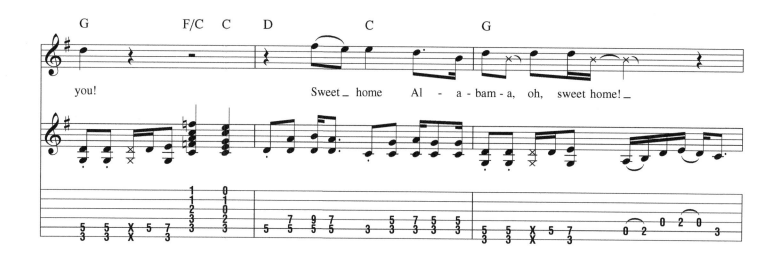

you!   Sweet _ home Al - a - bam - a, oh, sweet home! _

Where the skies are so blue, _ and the gov-'nor's true.   Sweet _ home Al - a-

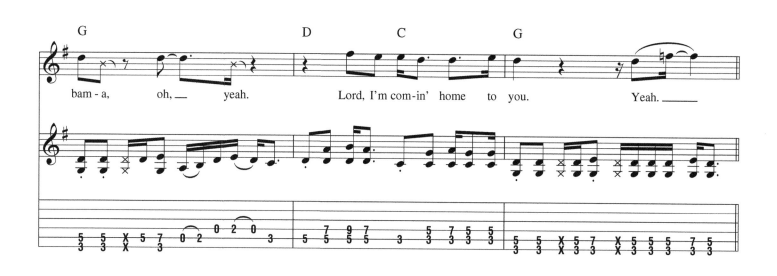

bam - a, oh, _ yeah.   Lord, I'm com-in' home to you.   Yeah. _____

Outro

Repeat and fade

Play 3 times

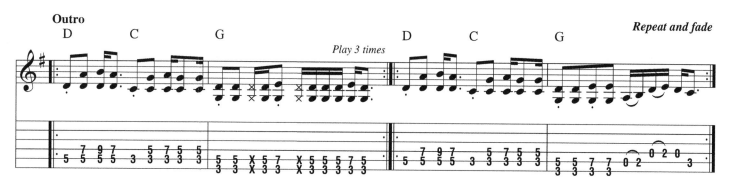

Tush

Words and Music by Billy F Gibbons, Dusty Hill and Frank Beard

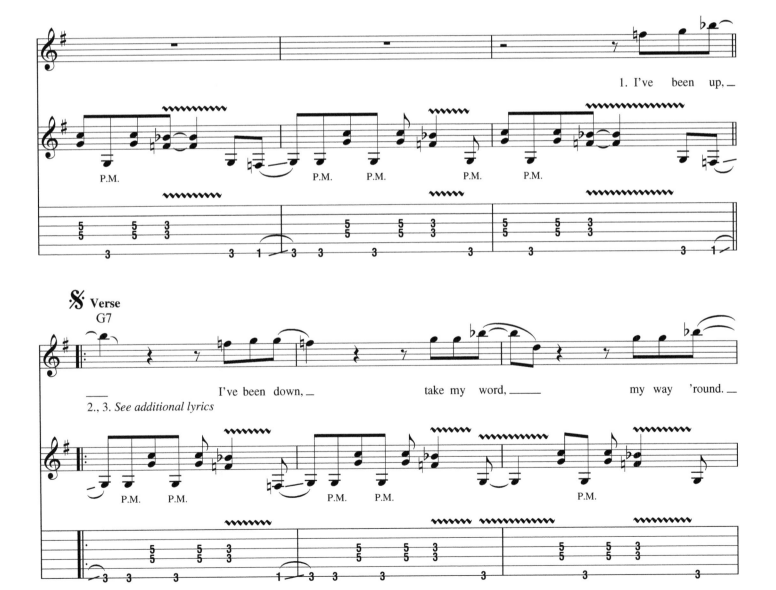

Guitar Solo

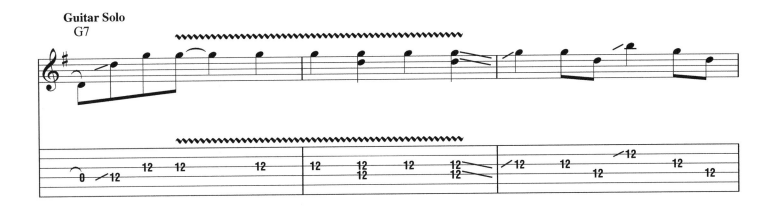

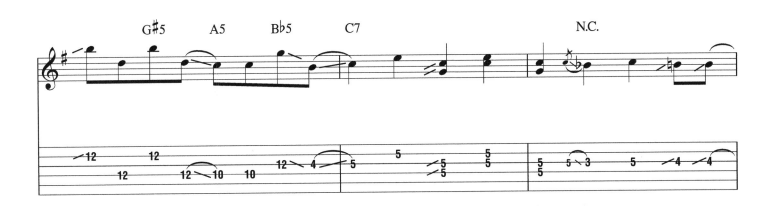

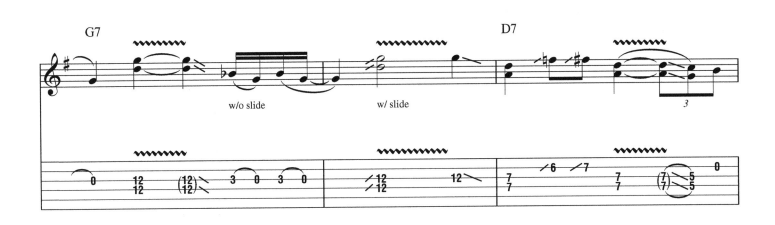

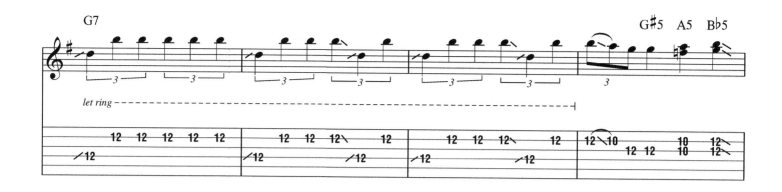

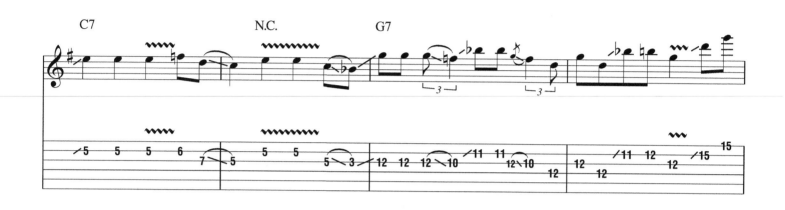

3. Take me back,

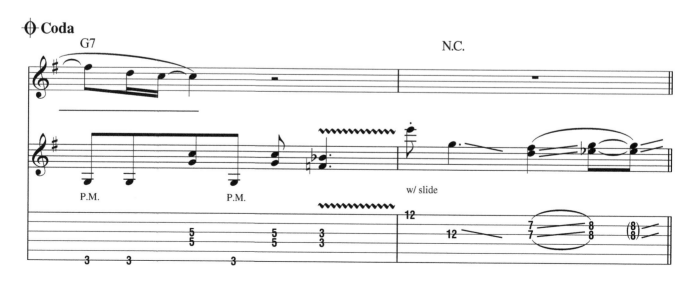

Outro-Guitar Solo

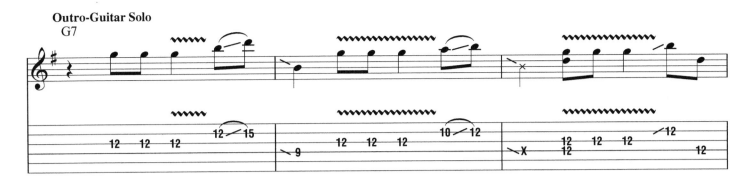

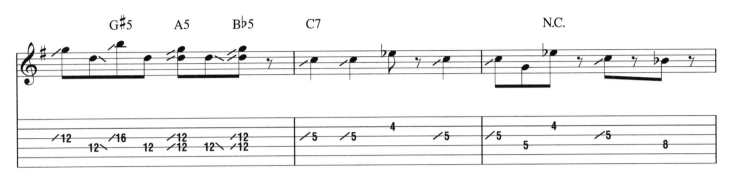

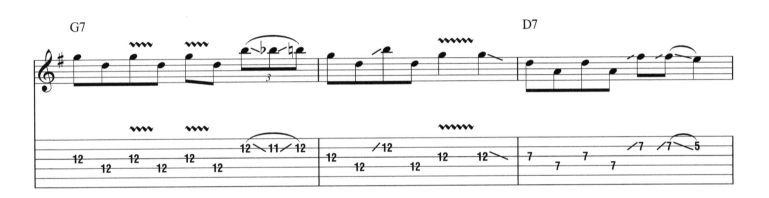

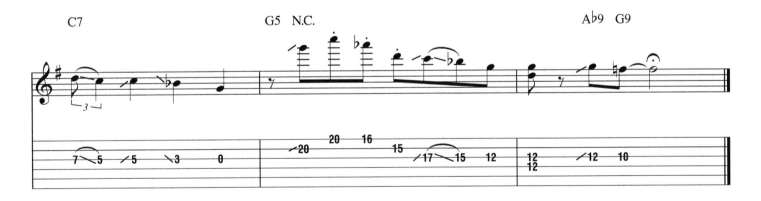

Additional Lyrics

2. I've been bad, I've been good,
   Dallas, Texas, Hollywood.
   I ain't askin' for much. Mm.
   I said, Lord, take me downtown.
   I'm just lookin' for some tush.

3. Take me back, way back home,
   Not by myself, not alone.
   I ain't askin' for much. Mm.
   I said, Lord, take me downtown.
   I'm just lookin' for some tush.

Talk Dirty to Me

Words and Music by Bobby Dall, Brett Michaels, Bruce Johannesson and Rikki Rockett

Tune down 1/2 step:
(low to high) Eb-Ab-Db-Gb-Bb-Eb

Intro

Moderately fast ♩ = 124

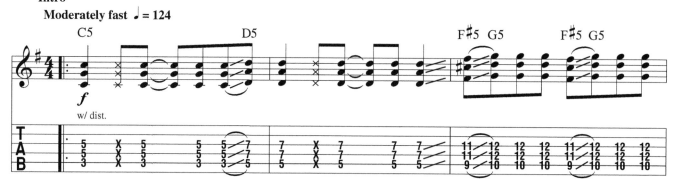

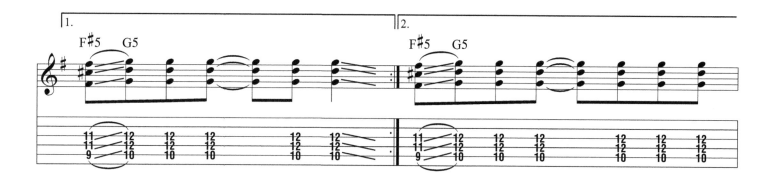

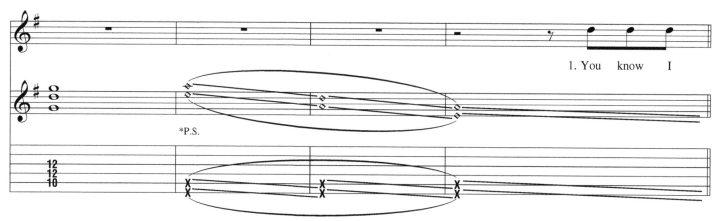

*Rub edge of pick down the strings, producing a scratchy sound.

Verse

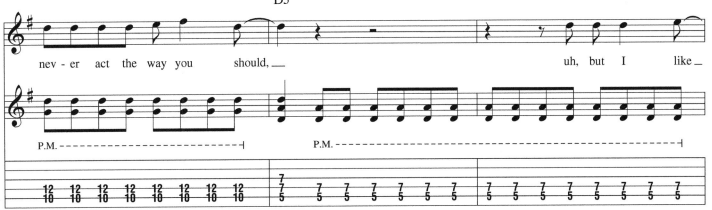

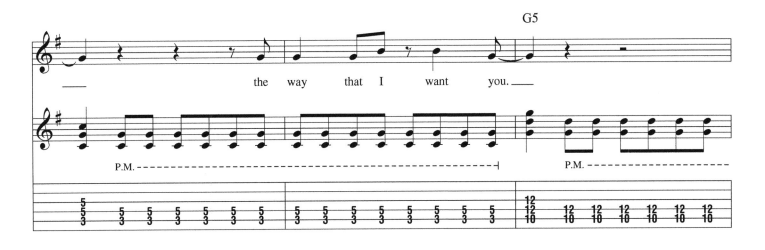

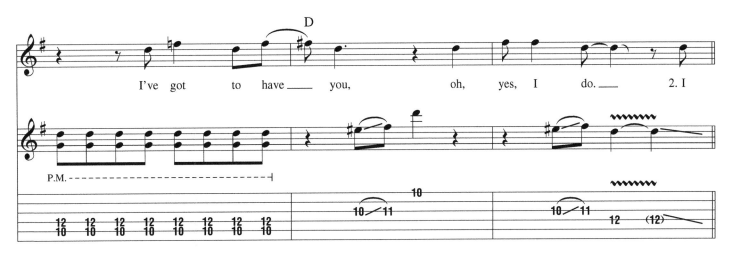

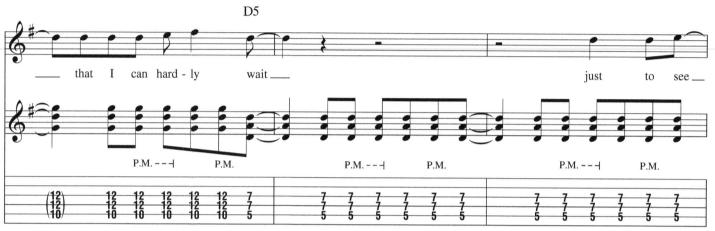

I got - ta touch ___ you. 'Cause ba - by, we'll ___ be ___

%‍ **Chorus**

at the drive - in, ___ in the old ___

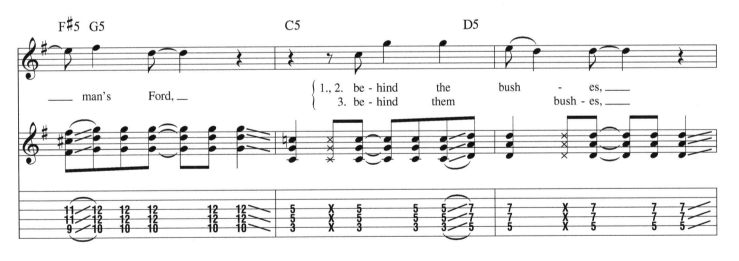

___ man's Ford, ___

1., 2. be - hind the bush - es, ___
3. be - hind them bush - es, ___

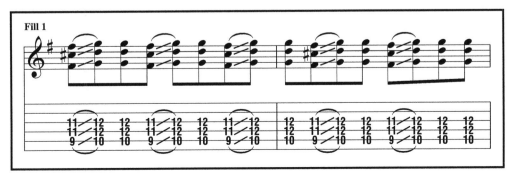

Fill 1

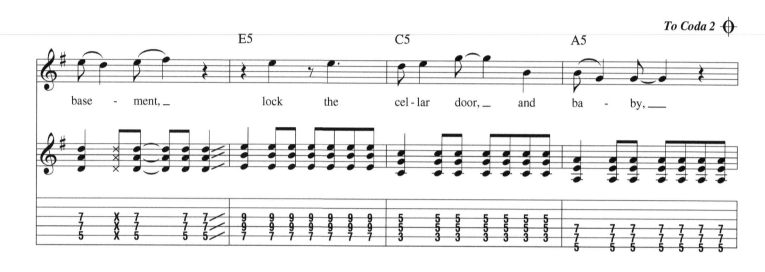

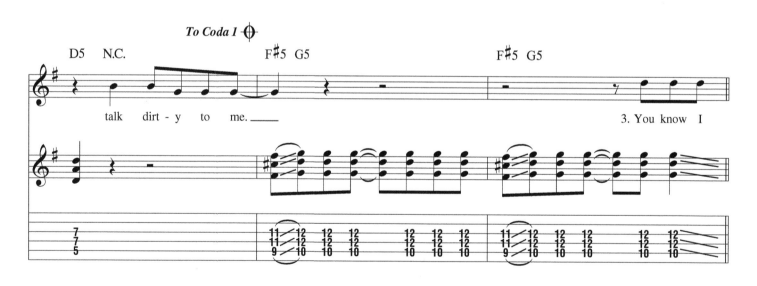

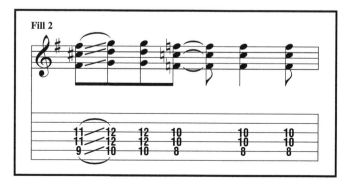

Verse

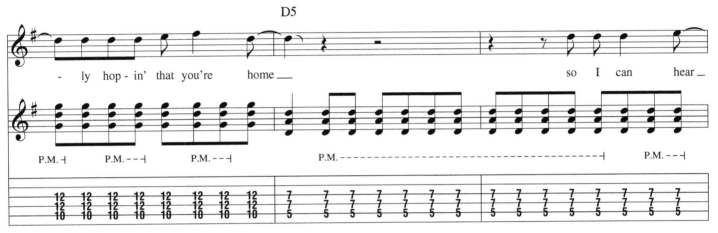

Coda 1

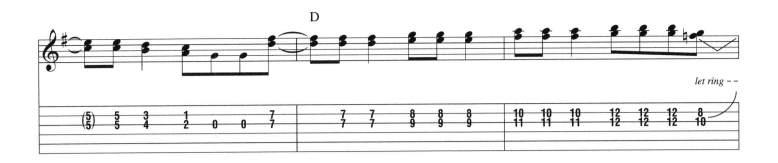

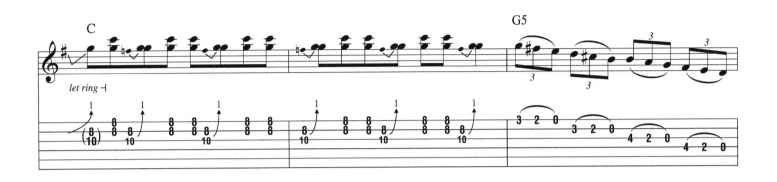

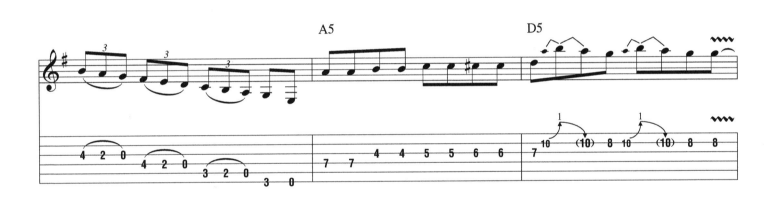

D.S. al Coda 2

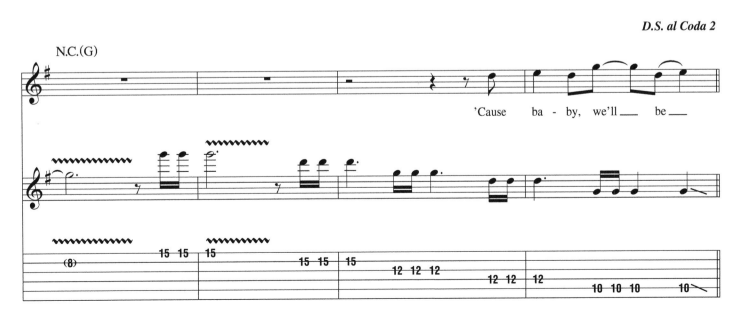

'Cause ba - by, we'll ___ be ___

Coda 2

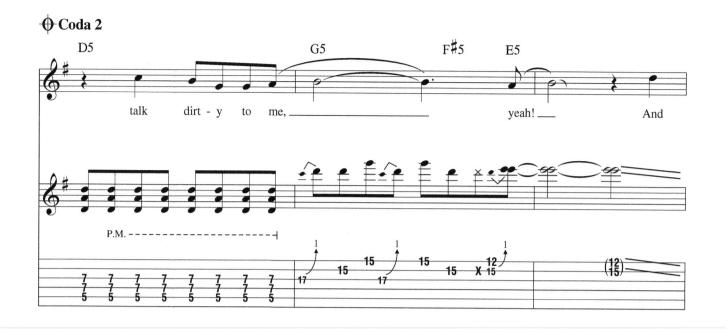

talk dirt-y to me, ___ yeah! ___ And

ba - by, ___ talk dirt-y to me, ___ yeah, yeah, yeah,

yeah. And ba - by, ___ talk dirt-y to me.

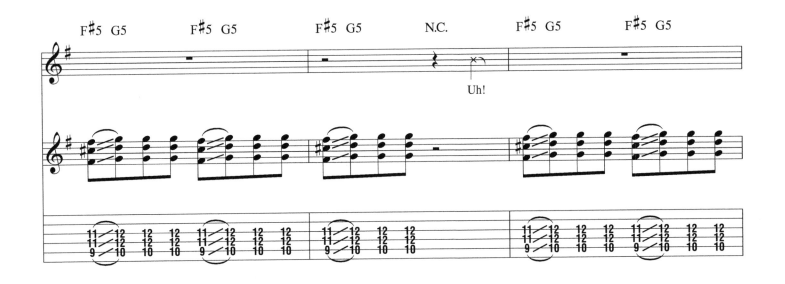

Free time

Woo!

That's the way I like it, baby.   Oo,   yeah.

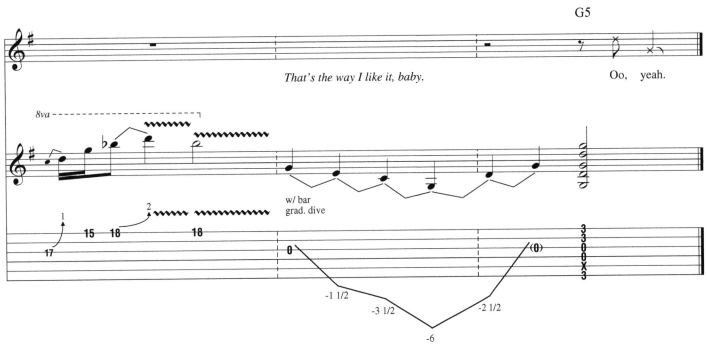

w/ bar
grad. dive

Guitar Notation Legend

THE MUSICAL STAFF shows pitches and rhythms and is divided by bar lines into measures. Pitches are named after the first seven letters of the alphabet.

TABLATURE graphically represents the guitar fingerboard. Each horizontal line represents a string, and each number represents a fret.

4th string, 2nd fret   1st & 2nd strings open, played together   open D chord

HALF-STEP BEND: Strike the note and bend up 1/2 step.

WHOLE-STEP BEND: Strike the note and bend up one step.

GRACE NOTE BEND: Strike the note and bend up as indicated. The first note does not take up any time.

SLIGHT (MICROTONE) BEND: Strike the note and bend up 1/4 step.

BEND AND RELEASE: Strike the note and bend up as indicated, then release back to the original note. Only the first note is struck.

PRE-BEND: Bend the note as indicated, then strike it.

VIBRATO: The string is vibrated by rapidly bending and releasing the note with the fretting hand.

PALM MUTING: The note is partially muted by the pick hand lightly touching the string(s) just before the bridge.

HAMMER-ON: Strike the first (lower) note with one finger, then sound the higher note (on the same string) with another finger by fretting it without picking.

PULL-OFF: Place both fingers on the notes to be sounded. Strike the first note and without picking, pull the finger off to sound the second (lower) note.

LEGATO SLIDE: Strike the first note and then slide the same fret-hand finger up or down to the second note. The second note is not struck.

SHIFT SLIDE: Same as legato slide, except the second note is struck.

TRILL: Very rapidly alternate between the notes indicated by continuously hammering on and pulling off.

TAPPING: Hammer ("tap") the fret indicated with the pick-hand index or middle finger and pull off to the note fretted by the fret hand.

NATURAL HARMONIC: Strike the note while the fret-hand lightly touches the string directly over the fret indicated.

PINCH HARMONIC: The note is fretted normally and a harmonic is produced by adding the edge of the thumb or the tip of the index finger of the pick hand to the normal pick attack.

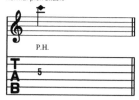

TREMOLO PICKING: The note is picked as rapidly and continuously as possible.

VIBRATO BAR DIVE AND RETURN: The pitch of the note or chord is dropped a specified number of steps (in rhythm) then returned to the original pitch.

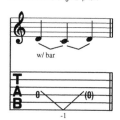

VIBRATO BAR SCOOP: Depress the bar just before striking the note, then quickly release the bar.

VIBRATO BAR DIP: Strike the note and then immediately drop a specified number of steps, then release back to the original pitch.

Additional Musical Definitions

(accent) • Accentuate note (play it louder)

(staccato) • Play the note short

D.S. al Coda • Go back to the sign ($), then play until the measure marked *"To Coda,"* then skip to the section labelled *"Coda."*

D.C. al Fine • Go back to the beginning of the song and play until the measure marked *"Fine"* (end).

Fill • Label used to identify a brief melodic figure which is to be inserted into the arrangement.

N.C. • Instrument is silent (drops out).

• Repeat measures between signs.

1.	2.

• When a repeated section has different endings, play the first ending only the first time and the second ending only the second time.

HAL LEONARD GUITAR METHOD

METHOD BOOKS, SONGBOOKS AND REFERENCE BOOKS

THE HAL LEONARD GUITAR METHOD is designed for anyone just learning to play acoustic or electric guitar. It is based on years of teaching guitar students of all ages, and it also reflects some of the best guitar teaching ideas from around the world. This comprehensive method includes: A learning sequence carefully paced with clear instructions; popular songs which increase the incentive to learn to play; versatility – can be used as self-instruction or with a teacher; audio accompaniments so that students have fun and sound great while practicing.

BOOK 1
00699010 Book Only.............................$9.99
00699027 Book/Online Audio $14.99
00697341 Book/Online Audio + DVD $27.99
00697318 DVD Only $19.99
00155480 Deluxe Beginner Edition
           (Book, CD, DVD, Online Audio/
           Video & Chord Poster) $22.99

COMPLETE (BOOKS 1, 2 & 3)
00699040 Book Only...........................$19.99
00697342 Book/Online Audio $27.99

BOOK 2
00699020 Book Only..............................$9.99
00697313 Book/Online Audio $14.99

BOOK 3
00699030 Book Only...............................$9.99
00697316 Book/Online Audio $14.99

*Prices, contents and availability
subject to change without notice.*

STYLISTIC METHODS

ACOUSTIC GUITAR
00697347 Method Book/Online Audio $19.99
00237969 Songbook/Online Audio $17.99

BLUEGRASS GUITAR
00697405 Method Book/Online Audio $19.99

BLUES GUITAR
00697326 Method Book/Online Audio (9" x 12") ..$16.99
00697344 Method Book/Online Audio (6" x 9")..$15.99
00697385 Songbook/Online Audio (9" x 12").......$16.99
00248636 Kids Method Book/Online Audio $14.99

BRAZILIAN GUITAR
00697415 Method Book/Online Audio $17.99

CHRISTIAN GUITAR
00695947 Method Book/Online Audio $17.99

CLASSICAL GUITAR
00697376 Method Book/Online Audio $16.99

COUNTRY GUITAR
00697337 Method Book/Online Audio $24.99

FINGERSTYLE GUITAR
00697378 Method Book/Online Audio $22.99
00697432 Songbook/Online Audio $19.99

FLAMENCO GUITAR
00697363 Method Book/Online Audio $17.99

FOLK GUITAR
00697414 Method Book/Online Audio $16.99

JAZZ GUITAR
00695359 Book/Online Audio $22.99
00697386 Songbook/Online Audio $16.99

JAZZ-ROCK FUSION
00697387 Book/Online Audio $24.99

R&B GUITAR
00697356 Book/Online Audio $19.99
00697433 Songbook/CD Pack $16.99

ROCK GUITAR
00697319 Book/Online Audio $19.99
00697383 Songbook/Online Audio $19.99

ROCKABILLY GUITAR
00697407 Book/Online Audio $19.99

OTHER METHOD BOOKS

BARITONE GUITAR METHOD
00242055 Book/Online Audio $12.99

GUITAR FOR KIDS
00865003 Method Book 1/Online Audio $14.99
00697402 Songbook/Online Audio $12.99
00128437 Method Book 2/Online Audio $14.99

MUSIC THEORY FOR GUITARISTS
00695790 Book/Online Audio $22.99

TENOR GUITAR METHOD
00148330 Book/Online Audio $14.99

12-STRING GUITAR METHOD
00249528 Book/Online Audio $22.99

METHOD SUPPLEMENTS

ARPEGGIO FINDER
00697352 6" x 9" Edition $9.99
00697351 9" x 12" Edition $10.99

BARRE CHORDS
00697406 Book/Online Audio $16.99

CHORD, SCALE & ARPEGGIO FINDER
00697410 Book Only..$24.99

GUITAR TECHNIQUES
00697389 Book/Online Audio $16.99

INCREDIBLE CHORD FINDER
00697200 6" x 9" Edition $7.99
00697208 9" x 12" Edition $9.99

INCREDIBLE SCALE FINDER
00695568 6" x 9" Edition $9.99
00695490 9" x 12" Edition $9.99

LEAD LICKS
00697345 Book/Online Audio $12.99

RHYTHM RIFFS
00697346 Book/Online Audio $14.99

SONGBOOKS

CLASSICAL GUITAR PIECES
00697388 Book/Online Audio $12.99

EASY POP MELODIES
00697281 Book Only..$7.99
00697440 Book/Online Audio $16.99

(MORE) EASY POP MELODIES
00697280 Book Only..$7.99
00697269 Book/Online Audio $16.99

(EVEN MORE) EASY POP MELODIES
00699154 Book Only..$7.99
00697439 Book/Online Audio $16.99

EASY POP RHYTHMS
00697336 Book Only..$10.99
00697441 Book/Online Audio $16.99

(MORE) EASY POP RHYTHMS
00697338 Book Only..$9.99
00697322 Book/Online Audio $16.99

(EVEN MORE) EASY POP RHYTHMS
00697340 Book Only..$9.99
00697323 Book/Online Audio $16.99

EASY POP CHRISTMAS MELODIES
00697417 Book Only..$12.99
00697416 Book/Online Audio $16.99

EASY POP CHRISTMAS RHYTHMS
00278177 Book Only..$6.99
00278175 Book/Online Audio $14.99

EASY SOLO GUITAR PIECES
00110407 Book Only..$12.99

REFERENCE

GUITAR PRACTICE PLANNER
00697401 Book Only..$7.99

GUITAR SETUP & MAINTENANCE
00697427 6" x 9" Edition $16.99
00697421 9" x 12" Edition $14.99

For more info, songlists, or to purchase these and more books from your favorite music retailer, go to

halleonard.com

HAL•LEONARD®

HAL•LEONARD® GUITAR PLAY-ALONG

Complete song lists available online.

This series will help you play your favorite songs quickly and easily. Just follow **INCLUDES TAB** the tab and listen to the audio to the hear how the guitar should sound, and then play along using the separate backing tracks. Audio files also include software to slow down the tempo without changing pitch. The melody and lyrics are included in the book so that you can sing or simply follow along.

Prices, contents, and availability subject to change without notice.

HAL•LEONARD®
www.halleonard.com